WHY. CAN'T. YOU.
BE. U.

WHY. CAN'T. YOU. BE. U.

GIOACCHINA INFANTINO

Story Terrace

Design StoryTerrace

Copyright © Gioacchina Infantino

First print November, 2022

StoryTerrace

www.StoryTerrace.com

Tellwell Talent
www.tellwell.ca

ISBN
978-0-2288-8923-6 (Paperback)
978-0-2288-8922-9 (eBook)

CONTENTS

DEDICATION

To my Beloved Twin Brother Anthony

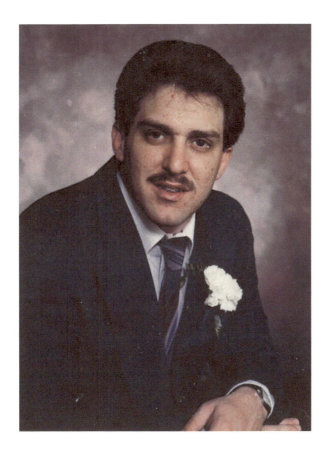

INTRODUCTION

I decided to write this book because I want to encourage you—especially women! — to learn how to be your true authentic self and find your ultimate potential in life. The earlier, the better. I want to dare you to drop your fears, insecurities, and any emotional blockages that are inhibiting you from becoming YOU.

In this book, I will explain how to uncover your layers and get to your essence by dropping the so-called invisible Emotional Mask most people live with. Becoming real can feel scary at first because you will be unlayering painful or undiscovered things about yourself, some of which you might have never explored before. Yes, this process will challenge you to go deep down into your core, but if you want to live an honest and happy life, there is no other way but through.

Once you bring to light and process these feelings, even the hardest ones, you can't imagine the many benefits and blessings that will follow! This journey will lead you to the right people, jobs, friends, and even professions, hobbies, and activities, which you've been always craving inside. You'll learn that there is nothing better than being you!

And remember, we live in an imperfect world with

imperfect people, so don't try to be perfect—just try to be the best you can be. Have the courage to drop your mask and put yourself first—your needs, your dreams—so you can walk down your destined road. Always be true to yourself. Nobody knows you better than you.

I hope the experiences and tips I share in this book will serve you as a guide and give you some practical ideas to start the process. It's never too late! I am still exploring myself—learning, unveiling, and unmasking to be a better me every day. Writing this book has helped me heal, and I hope it helps you too to meet your true self on the other side of the mirror. You can and will achieve this. I have been in your shoes, and I know you will come out on the other side with flying colors. We are all in a constant learning and healing process.

So strive to be you, respect yourself, enjoy the process, enjoy your achievements, and pat yourself on the back—not once but twice. You will never regret the work it took to get there. Please remember never to give up, no matter what the circumstances are because I can guarantee you that, at the end of your journey, you will see one big bright warm sizzling sun, which will comfort and guide you down your destined path. God bless you all. Thanks for reading my book. Please share your experiences with others, respect others in the process, and have an abundantly blessed life.

Love, Gioacchina

1

THIS IS ME, GIA

Gioacchina—Gia or Jackie for those who know me—is not the most common name. I was named after an Italian priest and missionary, Gioacchino La Lomia, to whom my mother was very devoted. I am a fraternal twin, born under the sun sign of Pisces, and I am also the youngest of four children. I have two older sisters and one beloved twin brother, Anthony. I love animals and have two sweet human-like cats named Charlie and Tony. I was raised in a strict and traditional Sicilian family in Queens, New York, and attended strict Catholic parochial schools, where I acquired even stricter rules. By the time I finished school, I was so frustrated that I wanted to completely escape from myself.

Bottled up

Growing up, I was obedient. I always did what was expected of me and never asked too many questions. My parents were honest hard-working people, who gave me all that was necessary: Food, shelter, protection, and love. But I have my brother Anthony to thank for the self-esteem and confidence I received at a very young age. When we were growing up, Anthony always put me on a pedestal and told me how strong and gutsy I was, and how proud he was of my strengths and talents. I was proud of him, too. He had a heart of gold, a pure genuine soul, and a great sense of humor. He accepted everyone for who they were. We supported each other in every way, and he always made me feel safe. During our school years, I always felt protective of him because he was very shy. I often had to speak for him around his teachers. Outside of our house, I always had the gift of the gab and was overly talkative, while he was quiet and reserved.

The only time we were apart was when he played sports after school, and I practiced singing on my tape recorder. I always loved to sing and dreamed of performing in front of an audience one day. Then we would always do our homework together after supper. He gave me the answers to the math exercises, and I helped him write his English compositions. The teachers never told us that they knew about our little system the whole time. It is true what they say—there is a magical connection between twins, and they always share secrets nobody else knows about. Every birthday, we blew our candles out together, side by side, and I never knew what loneliness was until he passed away 12 years ago.

Music to My Ears

My two older sisters, Lillian and Marie, lived at home until they turned 21. Then they flew off, got married, and had children of their own. When they were around, they spoiled me and bought me lots of gifts, but the best gift they ever gave me was a bit of freedom and music. When I was 13, I started attending Italian community dances with them. Of course, I was underage, but luckily I was chaperoned by my brother-in-law Tony and my sister Marie. I would never have had the opportunity to dance and sing with other people if it wasn't for them. I was so excited to be on a dance floor surrounded by bright flashing lights, loud rhythms, and romantic lyrics—people of all ages smiling, singing, and laughing. This brought out my outgoing personality and multiplied my love for music by a thousand. I was so happy to be away from the strict environment at home, where I felt so constrained, like a sealed bottle about to burst.

Unfortunately, my social and dancing privileges only lasted a while. A year later, at my first dance place, my sister and brother-in-law announced they were expecting their first child and would not be chaperoning me anymore. I was devastated. No more dancing, no more freedom. Back to the house of rules!

The Masking Years

After my sisters got married and left, I felt a huge void, an emptiness, I then returned back to my silent and obedient behavior. I was wearing an invisible mask. On the outside, I was wearing a people-pleasing mask for my family, my teachers, the nuns, and even for myself, to cope with the emptiness and constraints I felt. But inside I was yearning to be free and run out of the house, especially at night. Being home when it was dark and quiet depressed me terribly. I wanted to be working on the night shift to enjoy the bright lights, in the hospital and hallways, as well as the outside surrounding well-lit, multiple parking lots.

I worked very hard. It was an exhausting profession, but I loved it. I cared for 10 patients each night, attending to all their physical and medical needs. During those years, I never put myself first. Even in my personal life, I always felt I had to say yes to others, always yearning to please instead of doing what I really wanted to do—to sing. Sometimes I would get up in the middle of the night and sing quietly within the four walls of my room and pray out loud, "God, please give me an opportunity to break loose and sing." Music was always my release, a way out, a way of expressing myself, my happy and sad repressed feelings.

From Pain to Freedom

When I was 28, my father passed away, and the family dynamics changed. We were all grieving. I knew I wasn't happy, but I put off dropping my mask because I felt so many people needed me at that time. I could not stop pleasing. I felt my mom needed me to stick around to help and comfort her, so instead of fleeing and going on with my life like everyone else, I stayed home and focused on my careers—first as a Medical Assistant, then as a Child Care Technician for handicapped children, and lastly as a Licensed Practical Nurse. Helping my patients became an obsession. I had no intention of slowing down, but the universe had a different plan for me.

After years of stress, overworking, overpleasing, and never attending to my needs, I developed a painful muscle condition known as Fibromyalgia. Eventually, I had to withdraw from my nursing career due to the pain. From the moment I stopped working as a nurse, I slowly started to drop this false people-pleasing mask and took the first steps towards freedom and self-love. But it wasn't until I lost my brother and my mother that I really started to put myself first and do the inner work. I finally felt like my caretaker job was over, and now I needed to work on becoming my authentic self. My true self!

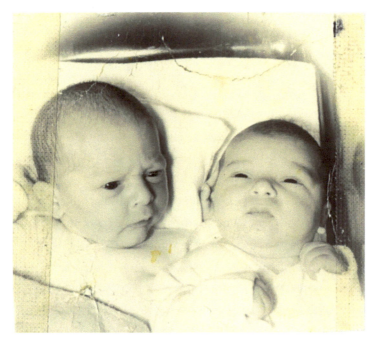

Twins (Birth Photo) - (Left) Anthony and (Right) Gioacchina

Nonna Maria (Baptism Day)

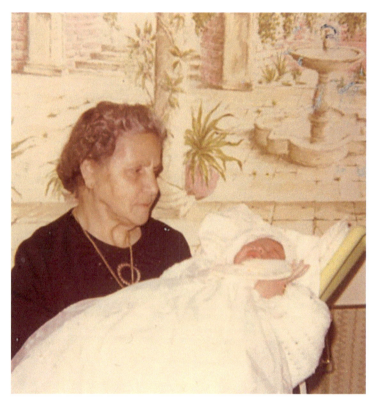

Nonna Maria (Baptism Day)

Miraculous St. Padre Pio

My twin/ buddy and me

Bonding with " Cookie", our first pet

My Nonno Filippo with his Daughter- (My Mamma) on her Wedding Day

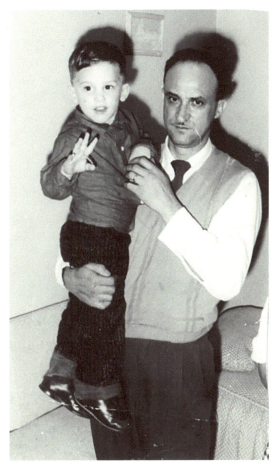

8-My Papa Calogero with son Anthony

*Mamma and Papa with my older sisters (Right) Lillian
and (Left) Marie*

Feeling Shy

Anthony's Grammar School Days

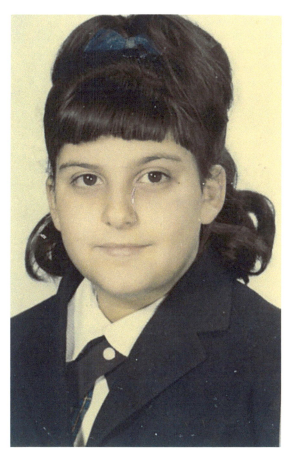

Gioacchina's Grammar School Days

Twins Confirmation Day

Celebrating High School Graduation with Parents

Twins Graduation

My Siblings and I

Twins Celebrating Birthdays Together

My Twin Anthony and Anne expecting their newborn son Charles

Anthony holding his son Charles

Photos of my Aunts and Uncles (Bottom) Mamma
I learned from them to never give up

Nursing Graduation Day with Parents

Nursing Graduation Day

My Outstanding Music Achievement

My Sweet Loving Cats (Right) Tony and (Left) Charlie

28 Home Sweet Home at Christmas

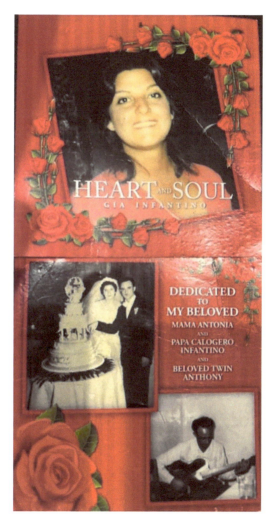

My 1st CD - Heart and Soul

Not For Selling Purposes, Family Dedication Gift

2

DROP THE FEAR, DROP THE EMOTIONAL MASK

What Is Masking?

I would like to introduce and discuss the art of Emotional Masking. Well, let's say, it's more of a coping mechanism than an art form. Emotional Masking consists of substituting one emotion or personality trait for another. For example, when a person acts like something is fine when it really is not, like saying you don't care about some issue when you really do care, or acting overly nice to someone when you really don't like them, or showing anger toward someone when the truth is you are hurting inside. Essentially, it is being someone else other than yourself—an impostor —wearing a fake layer, or mask.

Masking can begin as early as preschool years and get worse with age. After all, it is a socially learned behavior we get from our caregivers and the people around us when we're growing up.

Let's go back a bit! I would like to explain to you a little more about why people really feel comfortable masking. I would like to share one of my personal stories with you. Throughout the course of our lives, starting from the moment of birth to the present, people experience many feelings—good, bad, and everything in between—as well as traumatic events, such as death, divorce, accidents, illnesses, and more. As we coast through the years of our lives, we start to bottle up at least some of these emotions. Does anyone really talk about everything they experience in life, whether good or bad? No. They don't! And, because we don't talk about these emotions all the time, they remain "comfortably" buried. Or so we think. Let me give you an example—let me talk to you about grieving. When I lost my twin brother 12 years ago, this had to be the most devastating experience in my life. I always considered myself the stronger twin. I was the one that was not shy, talked a lot, and was always very social. On the other hand, my twin brother, Anthony, was shy, quiet, a little reserved, and not as social. Just knowing I had a twin made me feel safe inside. We shared every birthday from birth standing next to each other till the day God took him. I always felt I had an instant friend, not just a brother, but a life- long companion. And suddenly death! When he passed away, I felt like my foundation was pulled miles away from me, like I had no ground below my feet. My personality started to change. I was quiet, not as social, and for the first time in my life, I felt lonely. I never knew what loneliness felt like until his passing. Why did I mask my feelings then? I pretended that it was not happening because that was the only way I could cope at the time. Pretending not to feel lonely, placing my painful feelings in a deep, dark, and more bearable place. So you see, masking can sometimes be beneficial in times of emotional sorrow. It's when we don't deal with these feelings over a long period of time that they come back to haunt us, time and time again.

To truly heal, I needed to go deep within myself and think about all that was happening and all that had happened before his death. The day he passed, I had to give him CPR at home. It was unsuccessful. Being a nurse, I really thought I could bring him back. I was devastated. We were always together growing up, even though we had different social interests and activities—he loved playing basketball and baseball, and I loved dancing and singing. We always managed to join together at the end of the day for supper and to do homework. It felt great! What I'm trying to say is that my twin brother's death changed me. I had always felt secure and safe with him around. He always complimented me on my courage to get up and sing in front of people, my energy, and zest for life. When that was gone, I put on a mask that nobody saw but me, a mask that would cover my grieving. Behind that mask, I felt very lonely, torn inside, and wanted to just hide, be by myself, and feel he was still alive. I suffered from survivor's guilt. Keeping my invisible Emotional Mask on allowed me to cope with the outside world. Yes, inside I was in pain, but on the outside, I felt safe and secure, the two gifts my brother gave me.

Why Do People Mask?

Now that we have covered self-masking, I would like to explain to you why many people have a hard time removing their masks. We live in a world where people sometimes feel insecure and shy, and where people exhibit low self-worth and poor communication. People are afraid of continually being hurt and rejected. The reason is because these wounded souls have encountered negative people and experiences in the past. They then turned to masking as a way to protect themselves from this harsh painful world, which exposes us to anger, impatience, meanness, and intimidation. This is their way of protecting themselves. These people usually feel they need to put up a big defensive wall between them and the world so that they can protect themselves from being on the receiving end of repeated emotional pain.

Do you think it would be hard for these people to drop their masks? Absolutely! Some will go through life unintentionally aware of masking and never show their true authentic selves. Why? Because it works for them and because it's the only way they learned how to protect themselves. Others will be more authentic to themselves and experience the good as well as the bad by taking the risk to drop that wall. Why? Because it works for them and because maybe they learned from someone else that it is safe to be yourself. Either way, there is always a push–pull situation.

People do this to protect themselves from emotional pain, fear, anxiety, and rejection, and from being caught disguising their true selves. Masking is also used to conceal negative emotions, such as anger, sadness, frustration, anxiety, low self-esteem, guilt, or jealousy. When we feel hurt about something somebody did to us, instead of talking it out with that person, we bottle up our feelings. We feel angry, defensive, intimidated, and we go and put on a Protective Mask. People may sometimes think, *if I show people how I really feel, I will be rejected. If I open up and pour my heart out, I will be considered too vulnerable.*

For most of my life, I have been and still am a confident person, but I was a people-pleaser. I was a nurse, and I always put others first. I would have a pleasing mask on all the time, and by end of the day, I would be emotionally exhausted. I was masking! I was leaving my people-pleasing mask on to make everyone happy. I was not true to myself, and I was definitely not happy. I was not being me when I needed to be me; I was being who everyone wanted me to be instead. And let me just point out that even confident people wear masks. Wearing a mask does not only mean you are insecure, weak, or have low self-esteem. It just means you're not being you, and you feel a need to cover up something you just don't want people to see about you. It is a shame because there is something special about all of us, and wearing a mask inhibits the most talented and gifted people to not exhibit their best side.

People don't always wear Emotional Masks to protect themselves; they can also wear them to inflict pain on others. Let's see how.

For instance, if in the past you were very heavy, but you've lost weight. You've lost 50 pounds and look just great. A jealous enemy of yours just may say, "Wow! I have not seen you in long time. You gained so much weight!" Meanwhile, you just dropped 50 pounds and you're at your lowest weight ever. You look at this person, and they're smiling. Of course, you feel hurt because you know in your heart what they said is not true, and they said this deliberately to hurt you. They know they're hurting you and look happy because they accomplished what they set out to do. To hurt you! But you know sometimes people are unhappy with their own lives, and they look to sabotage people who are happy. Sometimes it's not only an evil friend—it can be a stranger, an acquaintance, a boss, or even someone in your family. Again, we live in a world with imperfect people. Everyone is going through their own process, and a lot of people are not even aware of why they do the things they do or say the mean things they say. They can be mean, selfish, jealous, and vindictive, and carry a mouth that can viciously ruin your reputation. Even when the malicious gossip is not true.

So, you see, anyone who wears a mask feels the need to cover up something—whether it be their insecurities and negative emotions, or untrue hurtful lies inflicted on other people.

The tempting thing about masking, and the reason why most people learn to do this in early life and carry on with it through adulthood, is that many of them never ever question why they do it or are even aware of it. This is because it can seem quicker, easier, and less stressful to keep a problem, a difficult emotion, or a challenge hidden, or pretend it's not there, than to face it. That's why Emotional Masking might seem comfortable or like an easy way out, at least for that moment in time when you're doing it. But in the long run, it doesn't help anyone—not you, or the people around you.

So, Why Demask?

I get it—it's scary to change. It's scary to reach out from under the covers, or from a small tightly closed box that you think has kept you safe all your life. That's why many people never leave a place like this, never ask themselves, *why do I cover myself up? Why do I hide my true feelings? Why don't I go for my real dreams?* As I said earlier, it can feel comfortable while you're doing it. It can seem easier than facing your truth, but, in the end, it's only destroying you. There is only one YOU, and there is only one life. You will never get this precious time back.

Also, you might be surprised by the amount of energy that covering your true feelings and wants requires. Emotional

Masking takes more energy than you think, and it can become very exhausting when used over a long period of time. And you've probably been doing it most of your life. It takes more energy to pretend you're someone else than to be yourself! That is why you may also experience a significant drop in masking, or even a complete drop, when you're sick. Being sick depletes your energy and lowers your defense mechanisms, like masking. But if you've been masking most of your life, chances are once you feel physically better, you'll go back to masking right away.

But the main reason why I recommend demasking is because if you continue to mask your negative emotions, you will never get to a point in your life where you are able to receive and manifest what God has waiting for you. If you go around like this, you will never thrive. You will never get that dream job, that promotion, that school you wanted to attend, meet that best friend, win that competition . . . Instead, you will go through life wearing a protective mask and being somebody you're not just because you experienced blows in your life that swung you to the ground. But you can get up. Get up!

Everyone in life wants to be happy. We all want to get up in the morning and say, "I hope that today I will have a good day." When we leave our homes in the morning, we do not know what challenges we will endure, what good things may happen, or what bad things. But we do know that we will put a mask on, in one way or another, to get through the day. If we wake up in a bad mood, we will try to cover it up, especially if we need to sit through that special meeting, if we are anxious to take a test, or go to that interview. We need to calm down and reduce anxiety so we can cope with the challenge. Boom! On goes our mask! Now we are ready. This helps us feel we have a better chance of acing our scores. Or when we feel hurt about something somebody did to us, instead of talking it out with that person, we hide that we feel angry, defensive, or intimidated, and we put on a Defensive Mask. This can go on for a very long time because, this is a hard mask to break.

Our cultural belief system can also cause us to self-mask. In some religions, it's disrespectful for women to speak over their husbands, or tell them what to do. Sometimes women have to be more submissive, or are not able to attend higher schooling and take on higher-income jobs and powerful positions in society. At least that is how it was many decades ago in Sicily, where my family is from. My dad used to tell me these were his parents' beliefs. These women who encounter barriers and limitations usually appear withdrawn, quiet, and introverted, especially when dealing with others in the wider world. So women are forced to self-mask to play this submissive role. On the other hand, there are other women who were brought up in cultures or traditions where women establish and run businesses and work in high positions, are strong in character, assertive, extroverted, and express their own opinions with males around them and in society generally.

We can't say either side is bad or good. What we do know is that we live in an imperfect world with imperfect people, and with a wide array of different types of Emotional Masks people use, the problem is how do these people wearing masks know when or how to be real?

They need to be real when they feel these masks have taken over their true identities. You need to show the world your true authentic self. This is where the problem begins. Does the person have the courage to show themselves in an imperfect world? You can do this, but first you need to fix yourself, the real you inside.

Don't be afraid to be you! We go through more than half our lives being someone else, being who our parents, siblings, friends, coworkers, spouses, community, and society expect us to be. Whether we are hiding behind our conformed culture and beliefs, wearing a false identity, a false inflated or deflated ego, false character, false image, role, or personality, we are still being robbed of our true authentic selves. Then, who are we? We don't know who we are. Not even if we pinch ourselves, can we feel the pain! We become deeply buried in several folded, creased, and convoluted layers of skin to the point where we cannot find our way out seeking that little crack in the skin. A crack that is so invisible it cannot be seen with the naked eye!

Are we conscious of what we are doing? What do you think? Are we blocking ourselves from finding out who we really are? Or is all this non-intentional? Let's find out! Well, some of us are already habitually accustomed to getting up every morning and repeating what we have already done for years. Doing what others expect us to, saying what others expect us to say, and the other nonverbal actions in between. Now, why do you think some people prefer or feel more comfortable going down that path? It's easier, less frustrating to oneself and others—it's a no-brainer, and what the heck? You are pleasing others; there's less confrontation, less friction. Well, at least that's what it appears like on the surface. So do you think people are sometimes afraid to be who they really are? And, if so, do you really think they can really be happy under the surface at the same time, while showing happiness or contentment on the outside? All this sounds pretty depressing, right? Don't worry cause a little later it will get better.

Being yourself, becoming yourself in the process of "unlayering", can be a real shock to others as well as to yourself. For some, it may mean having to shed all those tight comfortable layers of skin, which took years in the making. For some, it may mean uncovering years of hidden secrets, fears, inhibitions, dreams not manifested, and even past hurts and emotional wounds not dealt with in their childhood, teen years, adulthood, and even their senior years. For some, it can bring back and rehash triggered painful moments and situations of past trauma, deep scars, and insecurities not dealt with. Sounds scary, yes, but this does not mean that we all have deep-rooted past issues; it just means, for some, being afraid to be you can bring with it a little tag along. Baggage. Each of us is unique, so each situation is different.

Then there are some who are not interested in becoming their true authentic selves and are happy going along with whatever happens in their lives and are just "going with the flow." That's absolutely fine, but you would not be reading this book if you were not interested in bringing out your true authentic self.

3

HOW TO BE YOU—DEMASKING STEP BY STEP

Demasking is, as you might have guessed, removing one's invisible mask. People today in modern society are blocked by the suppression of their unaccepted emotions. And, as we learned in Chapter 2, Emotional Masking can also conceal embarrassment, disgust, disinterest, or different kinds of personal, societal, and business pressures.

If you've lived with a mask on most of your life, don't worry. It will be a commitment to break this masking habit. It's been said that it takes 21 days to break a habit and 60 to reinforce another. So be patient with yourself and with others in the process, and don't be afraid to say the word "no". Remember, you don't have to be a perfect mother, father, sister, brother, wife, husband, daughter, or son. Just be your authentic self with your limitations.

Self-love First

A healthy self-esteem and a good amount of self-compassion is the best (and only) place to start this journey. Please know that God made you special. There is only one DNA print of you in the world, and God does not make junk. What makes you think that other more aggressive, tougher, and more outspoken people are better than you? Nobody is better than you, and everyone is good at something. Remember we are all imperfect humans in this imperfect world, so if you can drop your mask, become who you were meant to be, and walk down your destined journey, you will have a fuller, more rewarding life.

To be honest, I have not dropped my masks 100 percent, nobody drops their masks 100 percent. I am still working on myself day by day, and that is OK! We are all a work in progress. So don't strive to be perfect, just be the best you can be. Cut yourself some slack, drop the masks, and be you. Nothing is better than being yourself, and it all starts with self-love.

Simple Techniques to Drop Your Mask

So what techniques can we use to drop this false Protective Mask, which is hurting us more than helping us? **We first need to admit to ourselves that we have a problem.**

56

1.**Self-awareness is the key!** It's just like anything else. Like wanting to stop drinking, smoking, eating unhealthy foods, or taking harmful drugs. Once you are consciously aware of doing something, you are ready to commit and change it. You get that green light! But you need to be able to get rid of that comfort space you put yourself in and be ready to feel that scary chill of change.

Let's face it—every time we cover something up, it feels good. For example, covering a cut with a Band-Aid, or even covering yourself with a blanket on a cold night. And just like that, we place a transparent mask over our face to feel safe, comfortable, and protected. Keeping this Emotional Mask on allows us to not deal head on with the emotional pressures that have been deeply buried for years, stop the triggers and traumas from coming back up to the surface, and forget the horrifying outcomes experienced.

Some people have more baggage than others, and some is more severe. Some simply started out for days and ran into weeks, months, and even years with no digging up to discover what's under the surface. So be patient with yourself and give yourself all time you need. You can do this. You can drop that invisible mask that has been haunting you all your life.

2.**Emotional history:** Here's a little exercise. Take a seat and try to go back as far as you can with your mind, trying to process your emotional history. Yes, this can be quite overwhelming; that is lots of history! But it will be worth it.

Maybe you can try to remember when something significant enough happened that emotionally scared you, hurt you, shocked you, confused you, deceived you, or made you feel betrayed. Bring up anything you can remember, and, if it helps, write it down on a list. Try to think about exactly what it was that you heard or saw to make you feel that way. Who was involved in this memory? How did you feel inside? How did the impact affect you? Did you feel the same emotions now remembering it as you did way back then? Do you still feel the same way now?

3.**Feel to heal:** Breathe and let this feeling of pain, trauma, shock, disappointment, sadness, or denial just settle over you. Don't try to push it away. Sit with this uncomfortable feeling and trust that you will be OK. Always remember you are not in that painful or sad situation anymore. You'll see that feeling of pain or fear as just that—a feeling. And it will pass just as it came. Trust me, it is way worse to pretend those feelings don't exist and hide them deep deep down in the dark or behind an Emotional Mask.

I myself have experienced trauma, pain, shock, and disappointment too. I am still healing, and if you are healing too, I can relate to that. I can relate to all of you. I am writing this book to heal along with all of you. Not until just a while ago did I realize that attached to my hip was a heavy bag of emotional baggage. Pain, betrayal, loss . . . . I could not go forward because I was repeating my negative patterns over and over. We cannot go forward if we don't forgive ourselves.

For years people wait for apologies, but they won't come in the way you want them. If people do say, "I'm sorry," I guarantee you, you will not be satisfied because it's not about them, it's always about YOU. What we need to do to be able to move on and truly heal is to apologize to ourselves, be compassionate to ourselves.

It took me half my life to realize that everything we need to heal is already inside of us. And if something happened in my life that went wrong, I definitely allowed it to happen somehow, even unconsciously. That is why they say wisdom is acquired at a more mature age. Turn to you, inside, and find the answers you need. They're there waiting for you to pause and listen to yourself. They were always there.

We turn to people for happiness and mask emotionally. We let grudges fester for years, fool others about the way we feel, rob our peace, and lose all the beautiful opportunities that were offered to us just because we feel more comfortable and safe wearing an Emotional Mask. Stop! Stop it! No more! Stand up, take charge. Feel those uncomfortable moments exposing yourself. Take these steps for as long as you need, until you start to feel the change.

Now go back to your list, and try to remember a similar difficult event from the first one that came to mind. Another circumstance or situation in which you felt any of those "bad" emotions, which maybe you can compare to other incidents on the list. I assume most of you have had at least more than one incident that impacted you emotionally. Take another piece of paper, and write down what these incidents all had in common. You just may discover these painful memories all made you feel the same. For example, a person that was abandoned in their childhood maybe decided—even unconsciously—to put on an Emotional Mask because they didn't want to feel vulnerable or weak. They might have wanted to show everybody on the outside world that they're strong and that they don't need anybody. Maybe even treat other people coldly as a defense. And the problem is they carried this pattern into their adult life, and now they have a hard time making friends or keeping a romantic relationship, and they don't know why.

See, once you are conscious of a behavior and its origin, you can change it!

And know that we are all in the same boat. We have all been in negative situations, and it does not matter whether you're masking or not masking. Fear, guilt, loneliness, anger, sadness, distrust, jealousy, anxiety, embarrassment, aggression, shame, boredom, frustration, envy, pride, worry, contempt, pity, sympathy, social rejection . . . . show me someone who hasn't experienced one of those!

As you can see, there are multiple negative emotions. At times we may even feel more than one at a time, and if you don't face them—if you pretend they're not there, they fester. They linger, they increase, they attack you, they control you, and then they paralyze you! You lose faith in yourself and feel like giving up. You think nobody understands you. Let me tell you something—you're wrong! If you only knew how many millions of people are in your situation. People get divorced, lose someone they love, feel alone, and withdraw from reality by using substances for a while. Then, when they get themselves together, they step out of the box again little by little, with baby steps. Just step out! Take your time, but just take the mask off, step out of the box and into this crazy wonderful world. And remember, you are not alone.

4.**Share your process:** People can help us heal. We don't have to do this on our own. Sometimes people can sit and listen to how you feel. It does not have to be a therapist, just somebody you can trust and feel safe with. Do you feel you can't trust anyone? Do you think everybody will ghost or ignore you? Well, I myself have felt ignored, and that is very painful, but there is always someone you can talk to, and by sharing important feelings and thoughts is how you can start to build trust in that relationship.

Now, sit with this person you can be transparent with and open up slowly. You don't have to tell them all the facts or details if you don't feel comfortable. Keep it short and to the point. Just open up and tell them the way it is. The way you felt. Did you feel lonely, abandoned, deceived, betrayed? Did you feel scared? Just express how this incident left you. You may realize something new. Maybe that you have been doing the same things over and over again and getting the same results. Why? Did we not learn from it cause it left us feeling confused? The truth is that you can't change something that you're not aware of, as I said before. If you've never processed these painful memories before, how could you understand them and get over them?

That's what I feel happened to me. We meet people in life who have issues. Some bestow on us intentionally, others unintentionally, and we never go back to process it. It was too painful, so we buried it.

Now that you have opened up and taken that step, how do you feel inside? Do you feel that maybe you can lower your mask a little? Now that you have taken the risk to expose what you were keeping hostage, you may feel lighter as well as happier. Good for you! Now you need to access what happens after you've lowered the mask a little and allowed some light to peek through. This process can take time. Be patient with yourself, but be bold, take the risk, and never give up. We will all heal at different speeds. It's like grieving. Grieving is painful; it's sometimes a shock, and it forces us to go back and remember things we don't want to. That's why Emotional Masking and grieving go hand in hand. Many of us are always grieving behind that Emotional Mask; I can relate to that type of pain also. Losing my mom and twin brother months apart left me devastated. I did not know who to grieve for each day. I wanted to honor them both.

Let's assume now that you lowered your guard a little, and some of the negative emotions you felt have left you. If they have not, give it time. Repeat the process over and over from steps one to four until you feel that you have gotten to a point where you can relate to others without having to cover up totally.

The last thing I want to tell you about removing your mask is to start to enjoy your progress, which leads us to the next step. Here's where the fun starts!

5. **Let yourself come out to play:** Use social activities and even little games to continue to explore your emotions and heal. In these technology-driven days, there are now online games and activities that can help you in this process of rediscovering yourself in a playful way. There's the *Feelings and Emotions game*, the Social Communications board game, feelings *Uno*, the *Empathy* board game, and *Roll and Spin!* (a coping strategy). These are just a few socioemotional games I discovered, which can help you explore your emotions and feelings. These outlets can bring us together with other people and encourage positive interactions by allowing us to let our guard down, be transparent, share laughter, communication, and trust, and develop a better self-esteem.

We can now feel more in control of our lives, and allow others to see our true selves. Once we are aware of what took us there in the first place, we can try not to repeat or have anyone sabotage our happiness and emotional growth in life. We need to learn how to love, respect, value, and appreciate ourselves first. We cannot allow other people who are wearing masks to interfere with our peace. We must not take what others say personally. What other people think of us is never about us—it is about them.

Give these steps a try, trust the process, and be kind to yourself. I do not think there is one person in this world who wants to wear an invisible mask forever. I understand there are times in your life when it might have seemed comforting, and that's fine! Sometimes we just want to say, "I'm hiding for a while. I'm not ready to face this." That's OK. The problem is when you lie to yourself and pretend everything is right when it's really just buried in the dark attic of your unprocessed thoughts and feelings. Only you hold the key to your attic, to your inner soul, and trust me, you can find so much freedom once you open it up and let some fresh air and light in.

I get it—life is full of pain, and taking your Emotional Mask off might make you feel scared, intimidated, and confused, at first. You may even feel like mentally running in the opposite direction. But you can do it! By taking it step by step when exposing your wonderful self to others, you will be surprised how you will start to change on the inside. Just have faith in yourself and watch your rewards unfold. A real transformation and life change are coming your way!

4

STRUT YOUR STUFF

Now you know that being real can be painful, but it will bring you down a lane that will lead you to encounter the right friends, the right job, the right situations, and a rewarding personal and even financial life. Yes! Being authentic is both painful and rewarding because it leads you to your true self, and there is nothing more wonderful than that.

By nature, we all are afraid of change. We are all scared of being ourselves. We all worry about how people see us. We are all afraid to show people our darker sides. We all have good days and bad days, good experiences and bad experiences. We all learn at different speeds and at different ages. We all want to be liked and accepted, and we all want to change, but many don't know how. We all are perfectly imperfect. I've learned that life is a journey of needles, pins, and rose petals.

Another lesson I learned in the process of demasking and finding my true self was to spend as much time as I could with people who had already dropped their masks and were living honest-to-themselves lives. That is, people who inspire you to be just you and who might already have accomplished what you dream to accomplish in your life. Let's say, deep down you've always wanted to be a writer; go find yourself a friend, a classmate, a teacher, or a mentor who has already published their writing, or someone who is making moves toward their goal and spend as much time as you can with them. Courage is contagious! So go get yourself some of that.

That is what I did. It took a lot of courage, but once I started to drop my mask and be true to myself, I decided to pursue my true passion for music and to sing again. I signed up to attend classes at the New York School for Music and took singing courses taught by Juilliard graduates. I always loved singing and remember my happiest dancing and singing years. But this was the time when I learned the basic breathing techniques and scales for the first time and took my singing to the next level. However, by then, I was moving into my mid-years and still longing to fulfill that empty emotional void inside.

Everything changed the day I walked into Cafe Italia, a local coffee shop in Whitestone, New York. I saw a man giving guitar lessons to the owner. As I walked in, I started singing Anne Murray's song "Could I Have This Dance?" and this man, named Eric Celerio, turned to me and said, "You sing?" and I responded, "Yes!"

From there on, I started taking classes, rehearsing, and making music with Eric Celerio—coach, musician, and producer. A car accident delayed my plans by six months, but I actually recorded two albums in two years under Eric's guidance and dedicated them to my beloved twin brother, Anthony, Mamma Antonietta and Papa Calogero. Most of the songs are classics, inspired by my brother's love of Elvis and the songs my father used to sing at home when I was a child. My first album is called Heart and Soul. My second album is called Gia Sings Elvis. Both albums are not for selling purposes. They are only family dedication gifts.

Now, who said miracles don't happen, or dreams don't come true? They sure do!

I am a perfect example. It's not easy to wake up every morning knowing, believing, and keeping the constant faith that your dream will come true someday, but I never gave up believing in my dream and in myself, and I urge you to do the same.

I want to thank my producer and mentor, Eric Celerio, for turning my long belated dream into a reality, and I fully encourage you to never stop believing in yourself and to go after your dreams, whatever they are, because miracles do happen.

Now enough of me! I hope my experiences and examples helped you understand the whats, whys, and hows of masking and demasking, and made you want to make a change in your life. After reading this book, you will learn to be proud of the person you have become, to be "you" without Emotional Masks. You will learn that it's OK to be imperfect without a mask, that people are not always who they claim to be while wearing their masks, when it's safe to mask, and when it's not. You will also notice how much emotional and mental freedom you have without masking your true self. You will learn that people will change only when they are ready and to never force anyone to do it if they don't want to. You will learn that it's OK to enlighten others by sharing your experience. You will encourage others to put themselves first. You will increase your self-esteem. You will teach others to have courage and lots of faith as they proceed in becoming themselves. You will tell them that being "you" is the best feeling ever and that you can leave your mask off. You will tell them not to be afraid to expose their layers and to be honest with themselves. You will tell them that being their true selves will bring them down a journey to who they were meant to be. You will know yourself better and emphasize your talents and the skills learned without masking. You will be complete. Congratulations! You aced this!

It takes time to be "you," but your ultimate goal is to reach your true authentic self and never stop being who you were destined to be. If this helped you, please encourage others to read my book so they can be enlightened and inspired to be themselves, too.

Go have an awesome life, and never ever give up. Never!

StoryTerrace

Printed in the USA
CPSIA information can be obtained
at www.ICGtesting.com
LVHW080753011023
759528LV00019B/11